CONTROLLED DRUG DELIVERY SYSTEM: A NOVEL APPROACH

Strictly as per P.C.I (R.G.P.V.) Syllabus Prescribed for B.pharmacy VII Semester

Ms. Komal Tikariya

B.Pharm, M.Pharm
Associate Professor
BM College of Pharmaceutical Education and Research, Indore
Madhya Pradesh, India

Mr. Shivam Soni

B.Pharm, M.Pharm
Assistant Professor
Shri Bherulal Pharmacy Institute, Indore
Madhya Pradesh, India

Mrs. Parul Raje

B.Pharm, M.Pharm
Pharmacist
Dept. of Public Health and Family Welfare, Bhopal
Madhya Pradesh, India

NOTION PRESS

This book is dedicated to our parents, family members, Collegues, friends and almighty god.

Contents

Controlled drug delivery systems: Introduction, terminology/definitions and rationale, advantages, disadvantages, selection of drug candidates. Approaches to design controlled release formulations based on diffusion, dissolution and ion exchange principles.Physicochemical and biological properties of drugs relevant to controlled release formulations

Polymers: Introduction, classification, properties, advantages and application of polymers in formulation of controlled release drug delivery systems.

Preface

This book describes current research on drug delivery system that encompass four broad categories namely: routes of delivery, delivery vehicles, payload, and targeting stretegies. When appropriate delivery vehicles and relevant release of specific agents in any of these categories in clinical application will be discussed. The chapter will highlight the Controlled, targeted, novel and individualized drug delivery encompasses the futuristic spectrum of pharmaceutical challenge to global health management. The regulatory agencies across the globe are also challenged to establish, standardize and implement the relevant requirements.

The main objective of the book is to explain the fundamentals of controlled drug delivery system in the simplest possible language, in an easy to understand way for the students. The textbook keeps a balance between the basic essentials and advanced areas of knowledge, apart from discussing the usual topics. it was found that very few such books were available.

This book will be very helpful to the academicians as well as the industry in understanding the concept of novel drug delivery system.

Ms. Komal Tikariya
Associate Professor
BM College of Pharmaceutical
Education and Research, Indore

Mr. Shivam Soni
Assistant Professor
Shri Bherulal Pharmacy Institute, Indore

Mrs. Parul Raje
B.Pharm, M.Pharm
Pharmacist
Dept. of Public Health and Family Welfare, Bhopal
Madhya Pradesh, India

Date: 11/06/2024

Acknowledgments

My gratitute and my sincere thanks to Mr. Umesh Kumar Atneriya for support and guidance throughout short of work.

Authors

Ms. Komal Tikariya

Mr. Shivam Soni

Mrs. Parul Raje

INTRODUCTION

Controlled drug delivery systems can include the maintenance of drug levels within a desired range, the need for fewer administrations, optimal use of the drug in question, and increased patient compliance. While these advantages can be significant, the potential disadvantages cannot be ignored like the possible toxicity or non-biocompatibility of the materials used, undesirable by-products of degradation, any surgery required to implant or remove the system, the chance of patient discomfort from the delivery device, and the higher cost of controlled-release systems compared with traditional pharmaceutical formulations. The ideal drug delivery system should be inert, biocompatible, mechanically strong, comfortable for the patient, capable of achieving high drug loading, safe from accidental release, simple to administer and remove, and easy to fabricate and sterilize. The goal of many of the original controlled-release systems was to achieve a delivery profile that would yield a high blood level of the drug over a long period of time. With traditional drug delivery systems, the drug level in the blood follows the in which the level rises after each administration of the drug and then decreases until the next administration. The key point with traditional drug administration is that the blood level of the agent should remain between a maximum value, which may represent a toxic level, and a minimum value, below which the drug is no longer effective.

TERMINOLOGY OR DEFINITION OFCONTROL RELEASE DOSAGE FORM

The United States Pharmacopoeia (USP) defines1 the modified-release (MR) dosage form as "the one for which the drug release characteristics of time course and/or location are chosen to accomplish therapeutic or convenience objectives not offered by conventional dosage forms such as solutions, ointments, or promptly dissolving dosage forms". One class of MR dosage form is an extended-release (ER) dosage form and is defined as the one that allows at least a 2-fold reduction in dosing frequency or significant increase in patient compliance or therapeutic performance when compared with that presented as a conventional dosage form (a solution or a prompt drug-releasing dosage form). The terms "controlled release (CR)", "prolonged release", "sustained or slow release (SR)" and "long-acting (LA)" have been used synonymously with "extended release".

Controlled drug delivery is one which delivers the drug at a predetermined rate, for locally or systemically, for a specified period of time.

Sustained Drug Release. Sustained release allows delivery of a specific drug at a programmed rate that leads to drug delivery for a prolonged period of time. Prolonged-release products release the active ingredients slowly and work for a longer time. A prolonged-release drug delivers a dose of a medication over an extended period of time. The prolonged release or sustained release systems, which only prolong therapeutic blood or tissue levels of the drug for an extended period of time, cannot be considered as controlled release systems by this definition. They are distinguished from rate controlled drug delivery systems, which are able to specify the release rate and duration in vivo precisely, on the basis of simple in vitro tests.

The difference between controlled release and sustained release, Controlled drug delivery- which delivers the drug at a pre determined rate for a specified period of time. Controlled release is perfectly zero order release that is the drug release over time irrespective of concentration. Sustain release dosage form- is defined as the type of dosage form in which a portion i.e. (initial dose) of the drug is released immediately, in order to achieve desired therapeutic response more promptly, and the remaining(maintenance dose) is then released slowly there by achieving a therapeutic level which is prolonged, but not maintained constant. Sustained release implies slow release of the drug over a time period. It may or may not be controlled release.

Drug targeting, on the other hand, can be considered as a form of controlled release in that it exercises spatial control of drug release within the body.

RATIONALE

The basic rationale of a controlled release drug delivery system is to optimize the biopharmaceutics, pharmacokinetics, and pharmacodynamics properties of a drug in such a way that its utility is maximized through reduction in side effects and cure or control of disease condition in the shortest possible time by using smallest quantity of drug, administered by most suitable route. The immediate release drug delivery system lacks some features like dose maintenance, controlled release rate and site targeting. An ideal drug delivery system should deliver the drug at a rate dictated by the need of body over a specified period of treatment.

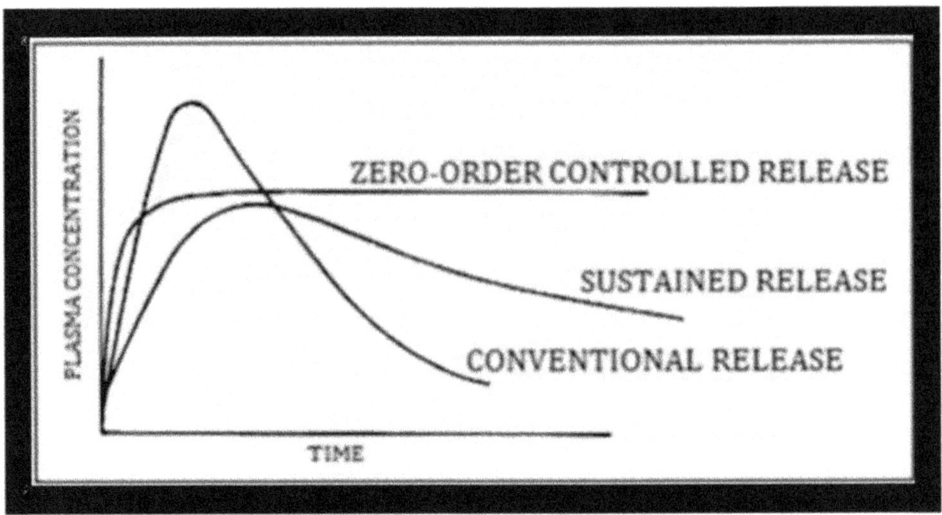

Fig. 1- Plasma drug concentration-time profile

Advantages of Control Release Dosage Forms Clinical Advantages

- Reduction in frequency of drug administration
- Improved patient compliance
- Reduction in drug level fluctuation in blood
- Reduction in total drug usage when compared with conventional therapy
- Reduction in drug accumulation with chronic therapy
- Reduction in drug toxicity (local/systemic)
- Stabilization of medical condition (because of more uniform drug levels)
- Improvement in bioavailability of some drugs because of spatial control
- Economical to the health care providers and the patient

Commercial / Industrial Advantages

- Illustration of innovative/technological leadership
- Product life-cycle extension
- Product differentiation
- Market expansion

- Patent extension

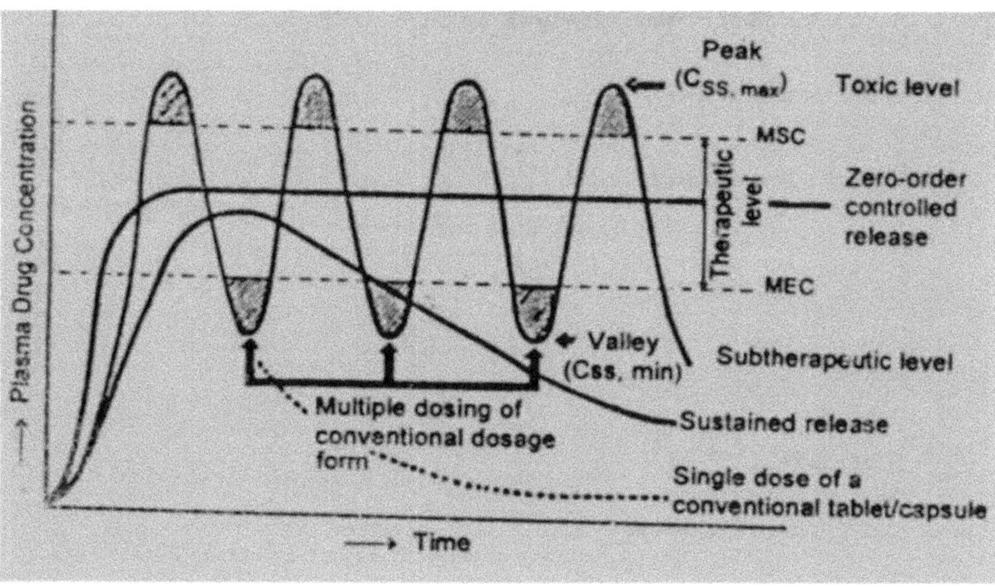

Disadvantages of CRDDS

- Delay in onset of drug action

- Possibility of dose dumping in the case of a poor formulation strategy

- Increased potential for first pass metabolism

- Greater dependence on GI residence time of dosage form

- Possibility of less accurate dose adjustment in some cases

- Cost per unit dose is higher when compared with conventional doses

- Not all drugs are suitable for formulating into ER dosage form

Selection of drug for formulation into extended release dosage form is the key step. Following candidates are generally not suitable for ER dosage forms

Selection of drug candidates or characteristics that may make a drug unsuitable for Control release dosage form

- Short elimination half-life
- Long elimination half-life

- Narrow therapeutic index
- Poor absorption
- Active absorption
- Low or slow absorption
- Extensive first pass effect

Parameters for drug selection

Parameter : Preferredvalue Molecular weight/ size: < 1000

Solubility: > 0.1 µg/ml for pH 1 to pH 7.8 Pka Non ionized moiety: > 0.1% at pH 1 to pH 7.8 Apparent partition coefficient: High Absorption

mechanism: Diffusion General absorbability: From all GI segments

Release: Should not be influenced by pH and enzymes

BIOPHARMACEUTIC AND PHARMACOKINETIC ASPECTS IN THE DESIGN OF CONTROLLED RELEASE PER ORAL DRUG DELIVERY SYSTEMS

Controlled release drug delivery systems are dosage forms from which the drug is released by a predetermined rate which is based on a desired therapeutic concentration and the drug's pharmacokinetic characteristics

Biological half-life (t ½)

The shorter the t ½ of a drug the larger will be the fluctuations between the maximum steady state concentration and maximum steady state concentration upon repetitive dosing. Thus drug product needs to be administered more frequently.

Minimum effective concentration (MEC)

If a minimum effective concentration, MEC is required either frequent dosing of a conventional drug product is necessary or a controlled release preparation may be chosen.

Dose size and Extent of duration

The longer the extent of duration the larger the total dose per unit delivery system needs to be. Hence there is a limitation to the amount of drug that can be practically incorporated into such a system.

Relatively long t1/2 or fluctuation desired at steady state

It is the belief of some that neither a SR nor a CRDDS is needed or useful for drugs having a t ½ of 12 hours or more. This is not so because there are two cases for which a 12 or 24 CRDDS seems to be indicated:

1. A drug having a t ½ between 12 and 72 hours may be designed for a CRDDS permitting application for every two to three days. The decline of the blood level time curve after release of the drug from the system will depend on the drug's t ½. Naturally, fluctuation between Css max and Css min may accordingly be relatively large in other words on adds slow release to the slow elimination process. For some drugs having a t1/2 between 20 and 100 hrs ,and which are intended for long term use

one may desire small fluctuations between peaks and troughs at steady

2. states either to achieve a certain therapeutic effect or because the therapeutic range is narrow.

DESIRED BIOPHARMACEUTIC CHARACTERISTICS OF DRUG TO QUALIFY FOR CDDS

Molecular weight or size

Small molecules may pass through pores of a membrane by convective transport. This applies to both, the drug release from the dosage form and the transport across a biologic membrane. For biologic membranes the limit may be a molecular weight of 150 and 400 respectively for spherical molecules and chain like compounds respectively.

Solubility

For all mechanisms of absorption the drug must be present at the site of absorption in the form of solution. During the Preformulation study it is necessary to determine the solubility of the drug at various pH values. If the solubility is less than

0.1 μg/ml (in acidic medium) one may expect variable and reduced bioavailability. If the solubility is less than 0.01 μg/ml absorption and availability most likely become dissolution limited dissolution limited. Hence driving force for diffusion may be inadequate.

It seems that drugs are well absorbed by passive diffusion from the small intestine upon per oral administration if at least 0.1 to 1% is non ionised form.

Apparent partition coefficient (APC)

Drugs being absorbed by passive diffusion must have a certain minimal APC. The higher the APC in an n-octanol/buffer system the higher is the flux across a membrane for many drugs. The APC should be determined for the entire pH range in the GI tract. The APC must also be applied for partition of the drug between CRDDS and the biological fluid.

General absorption mechanism

For a drug to be a variable candidate for per oral CRDDS, its absorption mechanism must be by diffusion throughout the entire GI tract. The term diffusion here refers to the dual pathway of absorption either by partitioning into the lipid membrane (across the cells) or by passing through water filled channels (between the cells). It is also important that absorption occurs from all segments of the GI tract which may depend on the drug's pKa, the pH in the segment, binding of drug to mucus, blood flow rate, etc. The absorption process seems to be highly dependent on the hydrodynamics in the GI lumen.

Even though that first order and square root of time release can result in highly effective drug delivery systems it is widely believed that the ultimate goal is zero order release profile.

Zero order release *invitro* release will produce zero order *in vivo* release and zero order *in vivo* absorption only if; (1) the entire GI tract behaves as a one compartment model, i.e. the various segments throughout the GI tract are homogeneous with respect to absorption, and (2) drug release rate is the rate limiting step in the absorption process.

With first order release on the other hand, smaller and smaller amounts are released per unit of time with increasing time. Assuming that rate of absorption gets slower past the small intestine due to increased viscosity, decreased mixing, and decreased intestinal surface area, less drug is absorbed.

In any case, the drug release from the CRDDS should not be influenced by pH changes within the GI tract, by enzymes present in the lumen, peristalsis, etc

For all practicality, the one compartment open model is quite suitable to design CRDDS for most drugs.

Pharmacokinetic parameters Elimination half life (t ½)

Drugs having a t ½ and 8 hours are ideally suited for CRDDS. If the t ½ is less than 1 hour the dose size required to be incorporated for a 12 hour or 24 hour duration dosage form may be too large. If the t ½ is very long there is usually no need for a CRDDS, unless it is simply intended for a reduction in fluctuation of steady state blood levels.

Total clearance (CL)

CL is a measure of the volume of distribution cleared of drug per unit of time. It is the key parameter in estimating the required dose rate for CRDDS, and predicting the steady state concentration.

Terminal disposition rate constant (Ke or λz) The terminal disposition rate constant or elimination rate constant can be obtained from the t ½ and is required to predict a blood level time profile.

Apparent volume of distribution (Vz)

The Vz is the hypothetical volume of a drug would occupy if it were dissolved at the same concentration as that found in blood. It is the proportionality constant relating the amount of drug in the body to the measured concentration in the blood.

Among the trio CL, Vz, and t ½, the former two parameters are the independent variables and the last one is the dependent variable.

The Vz or CL is required to predict the concentration time profile.

Absolute bioavailability (F)

The absolute bioavailability is the percentage of drug taken up into systemic circulation upon extravascular administration. For drugs to be suitable for CRDDS one wants an F value to be close to 100%.

Intrinsic absorption rate constant (Ka)

The intrinsic absorption rate constant of the drug administered peroral in the form of a solution should be high, generally by an order of magnitude higher than the desired release rate constant of the drug from the dosage form, in order to insure that release process is the rate controlling step.

Therapeutic concentration (Css)

The therapeutic concentrations are the desired or target steady state peak concentrations (Css max), the desired or target steady state minimum concentrations (Css min), and the mean steady state concentration (Css avg). The difference between Css max and Css min is the fluctuation. The smaller the desired fluctuation the greater must be the precision of the dosage form performance.

The lower Css, the smaller Vz, the longer t ½, the higher F and The less amount of drug is required to be incorporated into a CRDDS.

Approaches to design controlled release formulations

1. Dissolution controlled release
   - Encapsulation Dissolution control
   - Seed or granule coated
   - Micro encapsulation
   - Matrix Dissolution control

2. Diffusion controlled release

- Reservoir type devices
- Matrix type devices

3. Diffusion and Dissolution controlled systems

4. Ion exchange resins

5. Osmotically controlled release

MECHANISTIC ASPECTS FOR ORAL CONTROLLED RELEASE DRUG DELIVERY FORMULATION

Dissolution controlled release

Dissolution is defined as solid substance solubilized in a given solvent. It is a rate determining step when liquid is diffusing from solid. Several theories explain dissolution:

Diffusion layer theory, Surface renewal theory, Limited solvation theory.

Noyes Whitney Equation

$dc/dt = kD.A \ (Cs - C)$

$dc/dt = D/h \ A. \ (Cs - C)$

dc/dt = Dissolution rate, k= Dissolution rate constant (1st order), D = Diffusion coefficient/diffusivity, Cs = Saturation/maximum drug solubility, C =Conc. Of drug in bulk solution, Cs-C=concentration gradient, h =Thickness of diffusion layer.

Two common formulation system rely on dissolution to determine release rate of drugs are:

Encapsulated dissolution system (ii) Matrix dissolution system

Encapsulated dissolution system

This is also known as Coating dissolution controlled system. Dissolution rate of coat depends upon stability & thickness of coating. It masks color, odor, taste and minimize GI irritation. Controlled release products by decreasing the dissolution rate of drugs which are highly water soluble can be formulated by preparing appropriate salt or derivatives, by coating the drug with a slowly dissolving material, or by incorporating the drug into a slowly dissolving carrier. Examples: Ornade spansules, Chlortrimeto Repetabs.

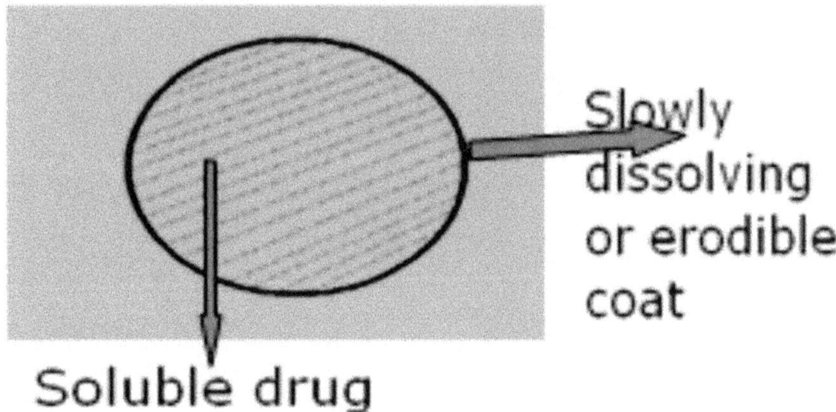

Matrix dissolution system

It is also known as monolithic dissolution controlled system. In this dissolution IS controlled by: Altering porosity of tablet, decreasing its wet ability, dissolving at slower

rate. It follows first order drug release. The drug release can be determined by dissolution rate of polymer. Examples: Demeaned extencaps, Dimetapp extentabs.

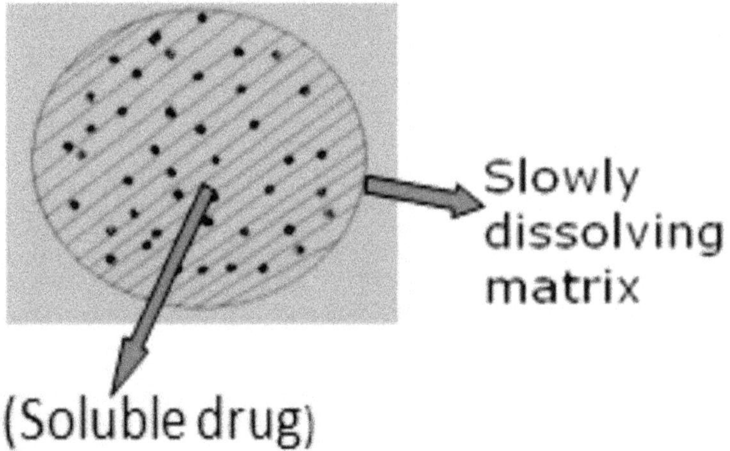

Diffusion controlled system

It is a major process for absorption in which no energy required. In this drug molecules diffuse from a region of higher concentration to lower concentration until equilibrium is attained and it is directly proportional to the concentration gradient across the membrane. In this system release rate is determined by its diffusion through a water-insoluble polymer. There are

two types of diffusion devices:

- Reservoir diffusion system
- Matrix diffusion system

Reservoir diffusion system

It is also called as laminated matrix device. It is a hollow system containing an inner core surrounded by water insoluble membrane and polymer can be applied by coating or micro encapsulation. The Rate controlling mechanism is that drug will partition into membrane and exchange with the fluid surrounding the drug by diffusion. Commonly used polymers are HPC, ethyl cellulose & polyvinyl acetate. Examples: Nico-400, Nitro-Bid.

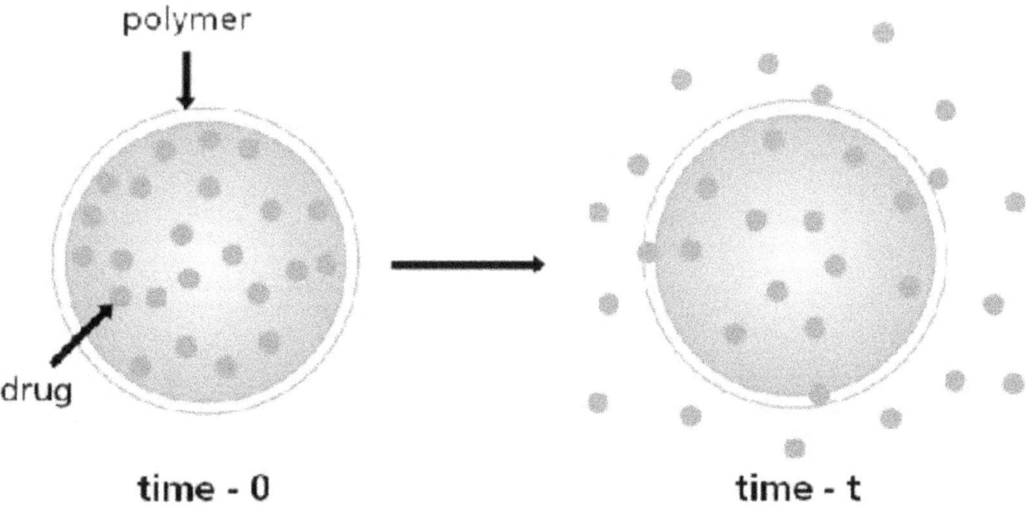

Rate controlling steps: Polymeric content in coating, thickness of coating, hardness of microcapsule.

Matrix dissolution system

(a) **Rigid Matrix Diffusion:** Materials used are insoluble plastics such as PVP & fatty acids.

(b) **Swellable Matrix Diffusion:** it is also called as Glassy hydro gels and popular for sustaining the release of highly water soluble drugs. Materials used are hydrophilic gums. Examples: Natural- Guar gum, Tragacanth.

Semi synthetic -HPMC, CMC, Xanthum gum. Synthetic -Polyacrilamides. Examples: Glucotrol XL, Procardia XL

The Higuchi Equation describing the drug release from this system [1]

: $Q = [D\mathcal{E}/T (2A-\mathcal{E} Cs.t)] 1/2$ Where Q=amt of drug release per unit surface area at time t, D=diffusion coefficient of drug in the release medium, $\mathcal{E}$=porosity of the matrix, Cs=solubility of drug in release medium, T=tortuosity of matrix, A=concentration of drug present in matrix per unit volume.

Rate controlling step: Diffusion of dissolved drug in matrix.

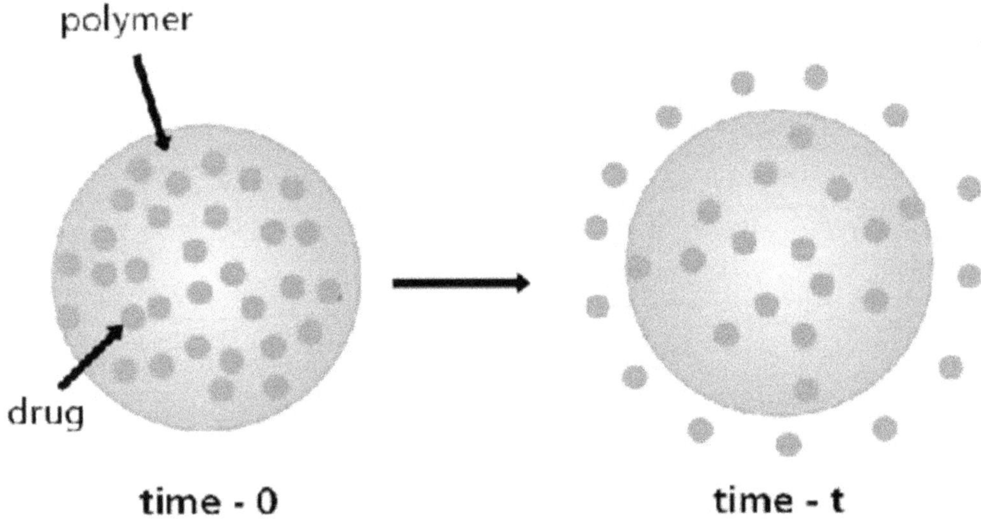

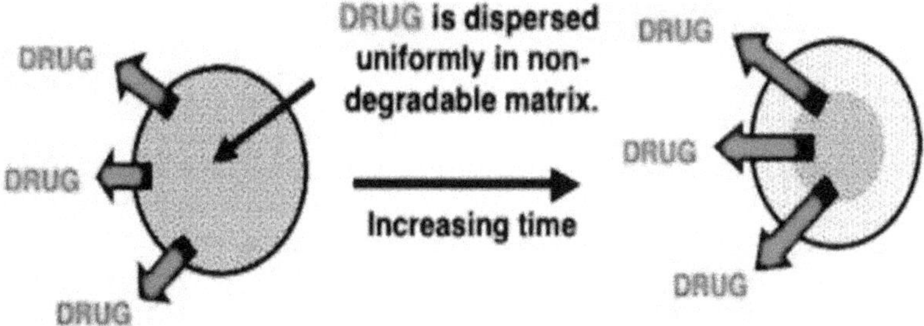

Dissolution & Diffusion Controlled Release system

In this drug is encased in a partially soluble membrane and pores are created due to dissolution of parts of membrane. It permits entry of aqueous medium into core & drug is dissolved or diffused out of the system. Ex- Ethyl cellulose & PVP mixture dissolves in water & creates pores of insoluble ethyl cellulose

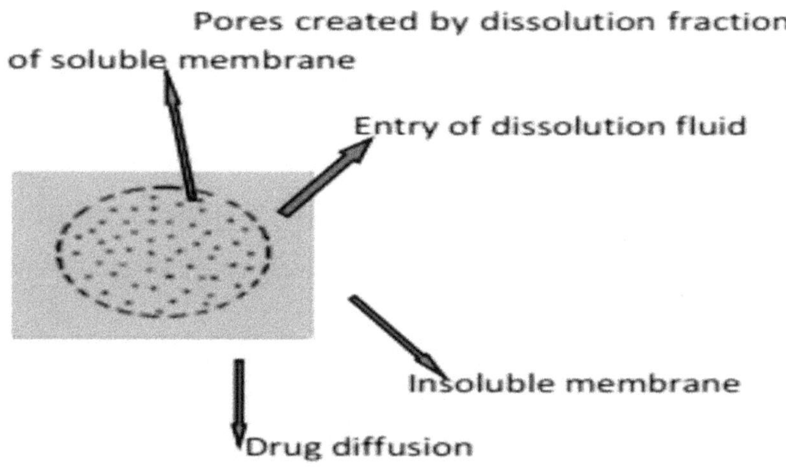

Ion exchange resins controlled release system

Ion exchange resins are cross-linked water insoluble polymers carrying ionizable functional groups. These resins are used for taste masking and controlled release system. The formulations are developed by embedding the drug molecules in the ion-exchange resin matrix and this core is then coated with a semi permeable coating material such as Ethyl Cellulose. This system reduced the degradation of drug in GIT. The most widely used and safe ion-exchange resin is **divinylbenzene sulphonate.** In tablet formulations ion-exchange resins have been used as disintegrant.

TABLE 1: Marketed drug products with their mechanism based classification

S.No.	Technology		Brand name	Drug	Manufacturer
1.	Diffusion controlled system		Welbutrin XL	Bupropion	GlaxoSmithKline
2.	Matrix system tablet		Ambien CR	Zolpidem tartarate	Sanofi-Aventis
3.	Method using ion exchange resin		Tussionex Pennkinetics ER suspension	Hydrocodon Polistirex and Chlorpheneramine Polistirex	UCB Inc.
4.	Methods using osmotic pressure	Elementary osmotic pump	Efidac 24@	Chlorpheneramine Maleate	Novartis
		Push-pull osmotic system	Glucotrol XL@	Glipizide	Pfizer Inc.
5.	pH independent formulation		Inderal@ LA	Propranolol HCL	Wyeth Inc.
6.	Altered density formulation		Modapar	Levodopa and Benserazide	Roche Products, USA

Principle:

Is based on preparation of totally insoluble ionic material

- Resins are insoluble in acidic and alkaline media
- They contain ionizable groups which can be exchanged for drug molecules
- IER are capable of exchanging positively or negatively charged drug molecules to form insoluble poly salt resinates.

Types:

There are two types of IER

Cationic Exchange resins - $RSO_3^-H^+$ Resins functional groups

Anionic Exchange resins – RNH_3^+ OH

Mechanism of action

IER combine with drug to form insoluble ion complexes

1. $R\text{-}SO_3^- \ H^+ + H_2N - A \rightleftharpoons R\text{-}SO_3 - NH_3^+ - A$

$R\text{-}NH_3^+ \; OH^- + HOOC - B \rightleftharpoons RNH_3^+ \; {}^-OOC\text{-}B + H_2O$

Where A- NH_2 is basic drug

B-COOH is acidic drug

These resinates are administered orally

2 hrs in stomach in contact with acidic fluid at pH 1.2

Intestinal fluid, remain in contact with slightly basic pH for 6hrs.

Drug can be slowly liberated by exchange with ions present in G.I.T

In the stomach

$®\text{-} SO_3 - NH_3 + - A + HCl \rightleftharpoons ®\text{-}SO_3 - H^+ + A\text{-}NH_3 + Cl^-$

$®\text{-}NH_3^+ Cl^- + HOOC\text{-}B \rightleftharpoons ®\text{-}NH_3^+ Cl^- + HOOC\text{-}B$

Undissociated Thus carboxylic acid will be poorly dissociated in stomach and thus absorbed.

In the Intestine

$® - - SO_3 - NH_3^+ - A + NaCl \rightleftharpoons ®\text{-} {}^-SO^3 - Na^+ + A\text{-}NH^3 + Cl^-$

Basic pH un dissociated

$®\text{-}NH_3^+ {}^-OOC - B + NaCl \rightleftharpoons ®\text{-}NH_3 + Cl^- + Na^+ {}^-OOCB$ Sodium salt of acid

(dissociation of acid salt unabsorbed)

Amine salt will be poorly dissociated in intestine and thus absorbed.

(3) CLASSIFICATION OF CONTROLLED RELEASE SYSTEM

The controlled release system divided into following major classes based on release pattern.

(1) Rate pre-programmed drug delivery system

(2) Activated modulated drug delivery system

(3) Feedback regulated drug delivery system

(4) Site targeting drug delivery system

(1) Rate pre-programmed drug delivery system:

In this, the release of drug molecule from the delivery system is pre-planed with particular flow rate profile of medicine. The system controls the molecular diffusion of drug molecules in or across the barrier medium within or surrounding the delivery system.

(1) Polymer membrane permeation controlled system

In this system, the drug is completely or partially encapsulated in a drug reservoir cubicle whose drug-releasing surface is covered by flow rate controlling polymeric membrane. In drug reservoir, the drug can be solid or dispersion of solid drug particle or concentrated drug solution in a liquid or in a solid type dispersion medium. The polymeric membrane may be made-up of the fabricated form of homogeneous or heterogeneous non-porous or partial microporous or semipermeable membrane.

(2) Polymer matrix diffusion-controlled system

In this drug, the reservoir is prepared by the homogeneously dispersing drug particles in the rate controlling hydrophilic or lipophilic polymer matrix. The resultant medicated polymer matrix provides the medicated disk with defined surface area and controlled thickness.

(3) Micro reservoir partition controlled system

The drug reservoirs are a suspension of solid particle in the aqueous solution of the water-miscible polymer. Micro-dispersion partition controlled system is prepared by the applying high dispersion techniques. In short reservoir and matrix dispersion forms micro-reservoir

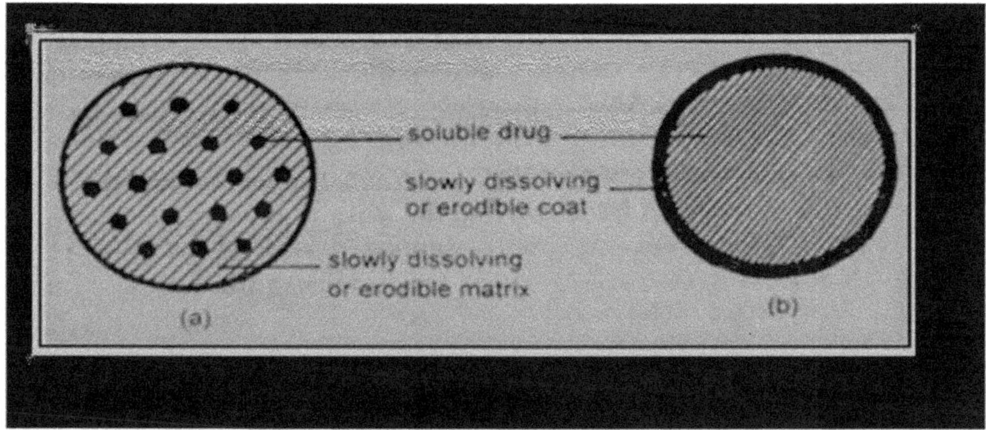

Fig. 3-Matrix and membrane type delivery systems

FACTORS INFLUENCING THE DESIGN AND ACT OF CONTROLLED RELEASE PRODUCTS

(1) Physiological properties

(1) Aqueous Solubility's: Most of the active pharmaceutical moiety (API) are weakly acidic or basic in nature that affect the water solubility of API. Weak water soluble drugs are difficult to design the controlled release formulations. High aqueous solubility drug show burst release followed by a rapid increment in plasma drug concentration. These types of drugs are a good candidate for CRDDS. The pH dependent solubility also creates a problem in formulating CRDDS. BCS class-III & IV drugs are not a suitable candidate for this type of formulations.

(2) Partition coefficient (P-value): P-value denotes the fraction of the drug into oil & aqueous phase that is a significant factor that affects the passive diffusion of the drug across the biological membrane. The drugs are having high or low P value not suitable for CR, it should be appropriate to dissolve in both phases.

(3) Drug pKa: pKa is the factor that determined the ionization of drug at physiological pH in GIT. Generally, the high ionized drugs are poor candidates for CRDDS. The absorption of the unionized drug occurs rapidly as compared to ionized drugs from the biological membranes. The pKa range for an acidic drug that ionization depends on the pH is 3.0 to 7.5

and for a basic drug it lay between 7 and 11.

(4) Drug stability: Drugs that are stable in acid/base, enzymatic degradation, and other gastric fluids are good candidates for CRDDS. If drug degraded in the stomach and small intestine, it not suitable for controlled release formulations because it will decrease in bioavailability of concern drug.

(5) Molecular size & molecular weight: The molecular size & molecular weight are two important factors which affect the molecular diffusibility across a biological membrane. The molecular size less than 400D is easily diffuse but greater than 400D create a problem in drug diffusion.

(6) Protein binding: The drug-protein complex act as a reservoir in plasma for the drug. Drug showing high plasma protein binding are not a good candidate for CRDDS because Protein binding increases the biological half-life. So there is no need to sustain the drug release.

(2) Biological factors

(1) Absorption: Uniformity in rate and extent of absorption is an important factor in formulating the CRDDS. However, the rate limiting step is drugged release from the dosage form. The absorption rate should rapid then release rate to prevent the dose dumping. The various factors like aqueous solubility, log P, acid hydrolysis, which affect the absorption of drugs.

(2) Biological half-life (t1/2): In general the drug is having short half-life required frequent dosing and suitable candidate for controlled release system. A drug with long half-life required dosing after a long time interval. Ideally, the drugs having t1/2 2-3 hrs are a suitable candidate for CRDDS. Drugs have t1/2 more than 7-8 hrs not used for controlled release system.

(3) Dose size: The CRDDS formulated to eliminate the repetitive dosing, so it must contain the large dose than conventional dosage form. But the dose used in conventional dosage form give an indication of the dose to be used in CRDDS. The volume of sustained dose should be as large as it comes under acceptance criteria.

(4) Therapeutic window: The drugs with narrow therapeutic index are not suitable for CRDDS. If the delivery system failed to control release, it would cause dose dumping and ultimate toxicity.

(5) Absorption window: The drugs which show absorption from the specific segment in GIT, are a poor candidate for CRDDS. Drugs which absorbed throughout the GIT are good candidates for controlled release.

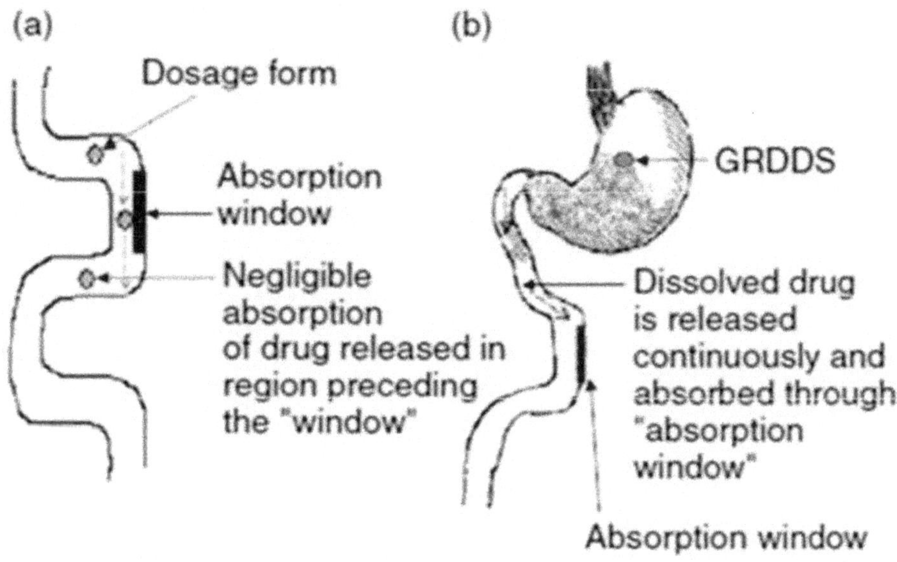

(1) Patient physiology: The Physiological condition of the patient like gastric emptying rate, residential time, and GI diseases influence the release of the drug from the dosage form directly or indirectly.

Pharmacokinetic parameters consider during the drug selection listed as follow.

Table. 1-Pharmacokinetic parameters for drug selection

Parameter	Comment
Biological or elimination half-life	Should be between 2 to 6 hrs
Elimination rate constant(KE)	Required for design
Total clearance(CLT)	dose independent
Intrinsic absorption rate	should be greater than the release rate
Apparent volume of distribution (Vd)	Vd effect the required amount of the drug
Absolute bioavailability	Should be 75% or more
Steady state concentration (Css)	lower Css and smaller Vd
Toxic concentration	The therapeutic window should be broader

2. POLYMER USED IN CONTROL DRUG DELIVERY SYSTEM

Polymers are becoming increasingly important in the field of drug delivery. The pharmaceutical applications of polymers range from their use as binders in tablets to viscosity and flow controlling agents in liquids, suspensions and emulsions. Polymers can be used as film coatings to disguise the unpleasant taste of a drug, to enhance drug stability and to modify drug release characteristics. The review focuses on the significance of pharmaceutical polymer for controlled drug delivery applications.Sixty million patients benefit from advanced drug delivery systems today, receiving safer and more effective doses of the medicines they need to fight a variety of human ailments, including cancer. Controlled Drug Delivery (CDD) occurs when a polymer, whether natural or synthetic, is judiciously combined with a drug or other active agent in such a way that the active agent is released from the material in a predesigned manner. The release of the active agent may be constant over a long period, it may be cyclic over a long period, or it may be triggered by the environment or other external events. In any case, the purpose behind controlling the drug delivery is to achieve more effective therapies while eliminating the potential for both under and overdosing.

POLYMERS AS BIOMATERIALS FOR DELIVERY-SYSTEMS

A range of materials have been employed to control the release of drugs and other active agents. The earliest of these polymers were originally intended for other, nonbiological uses, and were selected because of their desirable physical properties, for example:

- Poly(urethanes) for elasticity.
- Poly(siloxanes) or silicones for insulating ability.
- Poly(methyl methacrylate) for physical strength and transparency.
- Poly(vinyl alcohol) for hydrophilicity and strength.
- Poly(ethylene) for toughness and lack of swelling.
- Poly(vinyl pyrrolidone) for suspension capabilities.

To be successfully used in controlled drug delivery formulations, a material must be chemically inert and free of leachable impurities. It must also have an appropriate physical structure, with minimal undesired aging, and be readily processable. Some of the materials that are currently being used for controlled drug delivery include

- Poly(2-hydroxy ethyl methacrylate)
- Poly(N-vinyl pyrrolidone).
- Poly(methyl methacrylate).
- Poly(vinyl alcohol).
- Poly(acrylic acid).
- Polyacrylamide.
- Poly(ethylene-co-vinyl acetate).
- Poly(ethylene glycol).
- Poly(methacrylic acid).

Polymers:-

- Insoluble, inert - polyethylene, polyvinyl chloride, methyl acrilate, ethylcellulose.
- Insoluble, erodible – carnauba wax, stearyl alcohol, castor wax.
- Hydrophilic – methyl cellulose, hydroxyl ethyl cellulose, sodium carboxymethyl cellulose, sodium alginate.

In a matrix system the drug is dispersed as solid particle within a porous matrix formed of a water insoluble polymer, such as polyvinyl chloride.

Initially, drug particle located at the surface of the release unit will be dissolved and the drug released rapidly. Thereafter, drug partical at successively increasing distance from the surface of the release unit will be dissolved and release by diffusion in the pores to the exterior of the release unit.

The main formulation factor by which the release rate from matrix system can be controlled are; the amount of the drug in the matrix, the porosity of the release unit & the solubility of the drug.

However, in recent years additional polymers designed primarily for medical applications have entered the arena of controlled release. Many of these materials are designed to degrade within the body, few of them among these include:

- Polylactides (PLA).

- Polyglycolides (PGA).
- Poly(lactide-co-glycolides) (PLGA).
- Polyanhydrides.
- Polyorthoesters.

Originally, polylactides and polyglycolides were used as absorbable suture material, and it was a natural step to work with these polymers in controlled drug delivery systems. The greatest advantage of these degradable polymers is that they are broken down into biologically acceptable molecules that are metabolized and removed from the body via normal metabolic pathways. However, biodegradable materials do produce degradation by-products that must be tolerated with little or no adverse reactions within the biological environment.

These degradation products both desirable and potentially nondesirable must be tested thoroughly, since there are a number of factors that will affect the biodegradation of the original materials. The various important factors indicating the breadth of structural, chemical, and processing properties that can affect biodegradable drug delivery systems are listed below:

- Chemical structure
- Chemical composition
- Distribution of repeat units in multimers
- Presence of ionic groups
- Presence of unexpected units or chain defects.
- Configuration structure.
- Molecular weight.
- Molecular-weight distribution.
- Morphology (amorphous/semi crystalline, microstructures, residual stresses).
- Presence of low-molecular-weight compounds.
- Processing conditions.
- Annealing.
- Sterilization process.
- Storage history.
- Shape.

- Site of implantation.

- Adsorbed and absorbed compounds (water, lipids, ions, etc.).

- Physicochemical factors (ion exchange, ionic strength, pH).

- Physical factors (shape and size changes, variations of diffusion coefficients.

About Authors

Ms. Komal Tikariya B.Pharm, M.Pharm(Pharmaceutics) Has done the research Related Noval Drug Delivery System, Currently Working as an Associate Professor In BM College of Pharmaceutical Education and Research, Indore. She has 5 year of Teaching Experience.

Mr. Shivam Soni B.Pharm, M.Pharm (Pharmacology) Has done the research Related Herbal Form,ulations, Currently Working as an Assistant Professor In Shri Bherulal Pharmacy, Indore. He has 4 year of Working Experience.

Mrs. Parul Raje, B.Pharm, M.Pharma (Pharmaceutics) has worked on the research related to The Novel Drug Delivery System "Formulation and Evaluation of Solid Lipid Nanoparticle (SLN) based Topical of Ibuprofen"* currently working as Pharmacist in Department of Public Health and Family Welfare (Govt of MP) Bhopal Madhyapradesh. She has 1.5 yr industrial experience 1 year teaching experience and 6 year experience in public health care sector since 2016.

REFERENCES

1. Y.W. Chien. Novel drug delivery system. Volume 50.

2. John C, Morten C, The Science of Dosage Form Design, Aulton: Modified release peroral dosage forms. 2nd ed. Churchill Livingstone. 2002; 290-300.

3. Lee VHL. Controlled Drug Delivery Fundamentals and Applications: Influence of drug properties on design. 2nd ed. Marcel Dekker, Inc. New York: 1987; 16-25.

4. Modi Kushal, Modi Monali, Mishra Durgavati, Panchal Mittal, Sorathiya Umesh, Shelat Pragna. Oral controlled release drug delivery system: An overview. Int. Res. J. Pharm. 2013; 4(3):70-76.

5. Vyas SP, Khar RK. Controlled drug delivery: Concepts and Advances. 1st ed. Vallabh prakashan; 2002; 156-189.

6. Brahmankar DM, Jaiswal SB. Biopharmaceutics and Pharmacokinetics: Pharmacokinetics. 2nd ed. Vallabh Prakashan, Delhi: 2009; 399-401.

7. Allen LV, Popvich GN, Ansel HC. Ansel's Pharmaceutical dosage form and drug delivery system. 8th ed. 2004; 260-263.

8. Patrick JS. Martin's Physical Pharmacy and Pharmaceutical Sciences. 3rd ed. Varghese Publishing House. Bombay: 1991; 512-519.

9. Kar RK, Mohapatra S, Barik BB. Design and characterization of controlled release matrix tablets of Zidovudin. Asian J Pharm Cli Res. 2009; 2:54-6

10. Lachaman L, Liberman HA, Kanig JL.The theory and practice of industrial pharmacy. 3rd ed. Bombay: Varghese publishing house 1987.

11. Jain NK. Controlled and novel drug delivery. CBS publisher and distribution. 1997; 1-25.

12. Venkataraman DSN, Chester A, Kliener L. An overview of controlled release system. Handbook of pharmaceutical controlled release technology. Marcel Dekker Inc. 2000; 1-30.

9 7 9 8 8 9 4 4 6 5 4 0 1